LOVERS

Brian Friel

LOVERS

PART ONE:
Winners

PART TWO:
Losers

FARRAR, STRAUS AND GIROUX
New York

Published simultaneously in Canada by Ambassador Books, Ltd.,
Rexdale, Ontario

Printed in the United States of America

PART ONE

Winners

Cast

MAN
WOMAN
JOE
MAG

EPISODE 1

When the curtain rises, a MAN and a WOMAN are seated
on two high-backed chairs, one down left and one down
right, at the edge of the stage. They are the Commenta-
tors. They are in their late fifties and carefully dressed
in good dark clothes. Each has a book on his knee—not a
volume, preferably a bound manuscript—and they read
from this every so often. Their reading is impersonal, completely without emotion: their function is to give information. At no time must they reveal an attitude to their
material.

Between them and slightly upstage is Ardnageeha, the
hill that overlooks the town of Ballymore. For this I would
suggest a large pentagonal platform, approached by four
or five shallow steps all round. This is the only stage furniture.

MAG is seventeen, bubbling with life, inclined to be ex-
treme in her enthusiasms. Although she is not really very
beautiful, her vivacity gives her a distinct attraction.
Whatever she likes, she loves; whatever she dislikes, she
hates—momentarily. She is either very elated or very
depressed, but no emotion is ever permanent. She wears
a blue school blazer, white blouse, gray skirt.

JOE is seventeen and a half. He is a serious boy, a good

*student, interested in his books. He is at the age when he
is earnest about life; and he has a total and touching
belief in the value and importance of education.*

TIME: *The present in Ireland.*

MAN: At approximately 9:45 on the morning of Saturday, June 4, 1966, Margaret Mary Enright set out from
her home, a detached red-brick house on the outskirts
of the town of Ballymore, County Tyrone, Northern
Ireland. Before she left, she brought breakfast to her
mother, who was still in bed; and as she passed her
father's surgery, which is built as an annex to the
house, she tapped with the back of her fingers on the
frosted glass panel of the door. In a small attaché case
she had her schoolbooks and sandwiches for lunch.
She cycled through the town and at High Street she
met two friends and stopped to talk to them: Joan
O'Hara, a classmate, and Philip Moran. They told
her they planned to go boating on Lough Gorm that
afternoon and asked her to join them. She said that
perhaps she would. Then she cycled out the Mill Road
until she came to Whelan's Brae. There she left the
road and pushed her bicycle—

MAG *enters at this point.*

—across the fields until she came to the foot of Ardnageeha, the hill that overlooks the town of Ballymore.
She left her bicycle at the bottom of Ardnageeha, and
climbed to the top. It was a glorious summer's morning.

Temperatures were in the lower seventies. And there was no wind.

When MAG *gets to the top of the hill, she looks around for* JOE. *He has not arrived yet. She lights a cigarette, squats on the ground, and waits for him.*

WOMAN: At roughly the same time as Margaret Enright set out, Joseph Michael Brennan left his home at 37 Railway Terrace. His mother had gone to work two hours previously and had left his breakfast ready for him. His father was still in bed and asleep.

He went out through the back yard, down the mews lane, and across the waste ground between the rear of Railway Terrace and the railway line. On his way across the waste ground he met some children who were throwing stones at rats. He followed the line out past the marshaling yard, under the iron bridge, and for a mile out into the country. He carried his schoolbooks in a leather satchel. When he got to the level crossing he cut across the fields until he came to the foot of Ardnageeha, the hill that overlooks the town of Ballymore.

JOE *enters here.*

Then he climbed to the top.

MAG *sees him coming up the hill. She goes down the far side, i.e., up stage, until she is out of sight. There she hides.*

MAN: Margaret Enright was a pupil of Saint Mary's Grammar School, run by the Sisters of Mercy. And Joseph Brennan was a pupil of Saint Kevin's College, a grammar school for boys run by the clergy of the diocese. She was seventeen; he seventeen and a half. And they had their books with them because school was officially over for the year and they planned to spend the day studying for their final examinations at the end of their grammar-school course. The examinations began the following Wednesday.

JOE: Maggie! Maggie! (*Shouts*) Maaaaaag!

When he gets no response, he squats on the ground, opens his bag, takes out a book, and begins to work.

WOMAN: They stayed on top of Ardnageeha, that overlooks the town of Ballymore, from ten until two. They had their lunch up there. We can assume that they did some work because Joseph was an excellent student, not brilliant, but very keen and very industrious. Margaret was no scholar. She was intelligent but scattered. And we can assume that they talked some and perhaps dreamed some, because they were young and the day was beautiful. And even though the examinations were imminent, they cannot have been all that important to the young pair, who were to be married in exactly three weeks' time, on Saturday, June 25, because Margaret was pregnant.

JOE *glances up from his work and scans the land below him. No sign of* MAGGIE. *He returns to his book. Now*

MAGGIE *creeps up behind him and pounces on his back, trying to push him to the edge of the hill so that he will roll down. They wrestle for a few seconds.*

JOE: Come on! Cut it out, will you! That'll do!

MAG: Ha! You leaped like a rabbit!

JOE: I was looking for you. Where were you?

MAG: Waiting for you. You're late.

JOE: I was here at ten exactly.

MAG: I've been here for at least half an hour.

She throws herself on the ground in exaggerated exhaustion, produces cigarettes, and begins talking. During most of this episode JOE *is studying, or trying to study. But occasionally he tunes in to her prattle. By throwing in an occasional word he gives her the impression he is conversing with her.*

JOE: Did you walk it?

MAG: The bike's lying at the foot of the hill.

JOE: I didn't see it.

MAG: Sure you're half blind! God, my tongue's hanging out for a reek after that! (*Inhales and exhales with satisfaction.*) Aaaah, bliss! Sister Pascal says: You may search the lists of the canonized but you will search in vain for the saint that smoked. Maybe you'll be a saint, Joe.

JOE: Let's get started.

MAG: I read in a book that there are one million two hundred thousand nuns in the world. Isn't that fierce? Imagine if they were all gathered in one place—on an island, say—and the Chinese navy was let loose at them—cripes, you'd hear the squeals in Tobermore! I have a wicked mind, too. D'you ever think things like that, Joe? I'm sure you don't. I think that women have far more corrupt minds than men, but I think that men are more easily corrupted than women.

JOE: We'll get a couple of hours done before we eat.

MAG: (*With excessive disgust*) Food!—I don't care if I never see another bite ever again. My God, I thought I was going to vomit my guts out this morning! And this could keep up for the next seven months, according to Doctor Watson. The only consolation is that *you're* all right. It would be wild altogether if you were at it too. Sympathetic sickness, they call it. But it's only husbands get it. Maybe you'll get it this day three weeks— the minute we get married—God, wouldn't that be a scream! D'you know what Joan O'Hara told me? That all the time her mother was expecting Oliver Plunket, her father never lifted his head out of the kitchen

sink. Isn't it crazy! And for the last three days he lay
squealing on the floor like a stuck pig and her mother
had to get the police for him in the end. I love this
view of Ballymore: the town and the fields and the
lake; and the people. When I'm up here and look down
on them, I want to run down and hug them all and
kiss them. But then when I'm down among them I
feel like doing that (*she cocks a snook into* JOE's *face*)
into their faces. I bet you that's how God feels at times,
too. Wouldn't you think so?

JOE: I don't know how God feels.

MAG: Why not?

JOE: Because I'm not God.

MAG: Oh, you're so clever! Well, I'll tell you something:
there are occasions in my life when *I* know how God
feels.

JOE: Good for you.

MAG: And one of those occasions is now. (*Puffing her
cigarette regally.*) At this moment God feels . . . expansive . . . and beneficent . . . and philanthropy.

JOE: Philanthropic.

MAG: (*After momentary setback*) And we will not be
put into bad humor by grubby little pedants.

JOE: Look, Mag: we came up here to study. What are you going to do first?

MAG: French. And then maths. And then Spanish. And then English language and literature. And after lunch geography and the history of the world. I have planned a program for myself. The important thing about revising for an examination is to have a method. What are you starting with?

JOE: Maths.

MAG: Then what?

JOE: That's all.

MAG: Only maths?

JOE: Huh-huh.

She considers this absurd idea for a second. Then, because JOE *is wiser in these things than she, she readily agrees with him.*

MAG: Then that's what I'll do too. (*Really worried*) My God, if the volume of a cone doesn't come up, I'm scootrified! Not that I care—I can afford to go down in one subject. (*Pause.*) Joe . . .

JOE: What?

MAG: What's the *real* difference between language and literature?

JOE: You're not serious, Maggie?!

MAG: Don't—don't—don't tell me . . . I remember now . . . One is talking and the other is . . . books!

JOE: Talking . . . ?

MAG: That's it.

JOE: That's no definition! Language is—

MAG: Don't say another word. I have it in my head. But if you start lecturing, I'll lose it again. I have my own way of remembering things. Joe, last night again Papa asked me to let him get the flat painted for us before we move in.

JOE: (*Doggedly*)   I said I'll paint the flat.

MAG: That's what I told him. And I was thinking, Joe . . .

JOE: What?

MAG: If we put a lace curtain across the kitchen window, we wouldn't actually *see* down into the slaughterhouse yard.

JOE: And if we wore earplugs all the time, we wouldn't actually *hear* the mooing and the shooting!

MAG: (*Softly to herself*)   And even if a curtain did make the room darker, it'll still be lovely.

JOE: I signed the lease yesterday evening.

MAG: (*Absolutely thrilled*)   It's ours now? We own it?

JOE: Old Kerrigan was so busy working he wouldn't take time off to go into the office; so we put the document on the back of a cow that was about to be shot and that's where we signed it. Cockeyed old miser!

MAG: He's not!

JOE: What?

MAG: Cockeyed.

JOE: I'm telling you. And crazy, too. In a big rubber apron and him dripping with blood. And cows and sheep and bullocks dropping dead all around him.

MAG: Oh God, my stomach!

JOE *realizes that his tale is successful. He gets up on his feet to enact the scene.* MAG *listens with delight and soon gets drawn into the pantomime.*

JOE: "Drive them up there! Another beast. Come on! Come on! I haven't all day. And what's bothering you, young Brennan? Steady, there! Steady! Bang! Bang! Drag it away! Slit its throat! Slice it open! Skin it!"

MAG: Stop—stop!

JOE: "Another beast! Get a move on! What am I paying you fellas for?" You told me to call about the flat, Mr. Kerrigan. "Steady—bang! Bang! Damnit, I nearly missed—bang!—that's it. Drag him off. What are you saying, young Brennan? The lease? Oh, the lease! Oh, aye. Here we are." (JOE *produces an imaginary document from his hip pocket.*) "Best flat in town. Hell, it's all blood now." (JOE *wipes the imaginary document on his leg.*) "Come on! Another animal! There's a fine beast for you, young Brennan! Look at those shanks! Bang! Bang! Never knew what hit him! I sign here, son, don't I?" (JOE *pretends to write: but the pen does not work and he flings it away.*) "Hell, that doesn't write."

MAG: Bang! Bang!

JOE: "Keep behind me, young Brennan. This is a dangerous job."

MAG: Let's sign it in blood, young Brennan.

JOE: "Finest view in town. And the noise down here's great company. Bang! Bang!"

MAG: Like living in Dead Man's Creek.

JOE: There's a bullock that looks like the president of Saint Kevin's. Bang! Bang!

MAG: A sheep the image of Sister Paul. Bang! Bang!

JOE: Drag 'em away!

MAG: Slice 'em open!

JOE: Joan O'Hara's white poodle, Tweeny.

MAG: Bang! And Philip Moran's mother.

JOE: Bang! Bang! Doctor Watson.

MAG: A friend. Pass, friend, pass.

JOE: Skinny Skeehan, the solicitor.

MAG: Bang-bang-bang-bang! Look—reverend mother!

JOE: Where?

MAG: To the right—behind the rocks!

JOE: (*Calling sweetly*) Mother Dolores.

MAG: (*Answering sweetly*) Yes, Joseph?

JOE: (*Viciously*) Bang-bang-bang!

MAG *grabs her stomach and falls slowly.*

MAG: Into thy hands, O Lord—

JOE: Bang!

The final bullet enters her shoulder.

MAG: O shite—!

MAG *rolls on the ground, helpless with laughter.*

JOE: The town clerk—bang! All the teachers—bang!

MAG: The church choir—

JOE: Bang! Everyone that lives along snobby, snotty
Melville Road—bang-bang-bang-bang-bang!

MAG: A holy-cost, by God.

JOE *listens attentively. Silence.*

JOE: Everything's quiet. Now we'll have peace to study.
Back to the books.

MAG: I'm sore all over. (*Searching*) Give us a fag quick.

JOE: (*Bashfully*) I'm afraid—I—sort of—sort of lost my head there, ma'am.

MAG: Does your mother know you act the clown like that?

JOE: Does your father know you smoke? Look at the time it is! I came here to work.

He goes back to his books. He is immediately immersed.

MAG: Joe . . .

JOE: What?

MAG: The flat's ours now?

JOE: Isn't that what I'm telling you.

MAG: You're sure you wouldn't like the top floor in our house?

JOE: Positive.

MAG: (*After a moment's hesitation*) So am I. I just wanted to know if you were, too.

JOE: Goodbye.

MAG: It's only that Papa'll be lonely without me. For his sake, really. But he'll get over that. And it's just that this is the first time he'll ever have been separated from me, even for a night. But he'll get over it. All parents have to face it sooner or later. (*Happily*) Besides, I can wheel the pram over every afternoon. (*She looks at* JOE, *lost in his books: and again she has the momentary dread of the exam.*) I'm like you, Joe. When I concentrate, you could yell at me and I wouldn't hear you.

She opens a book—almost at random. Looks at the sky.

It's going to be very warm . . .

She takes off her school blazer, rolls up the sleeves of her blouse, and stretches out under the sun.

If we didn't have to work, we could sun-bathe.

Pause.

MAG: That Easter we were in Florence, I kept thinking about your father and how good the sun there would have been for his asthma. I read in a book that asthma is purely psychosomatic and that a man with asthma has a mother-fixation. Crazy the things they dig up too. I'm glad Papa's not a doctor or he'd be watching me for symptoms all the time. Your parents are such wonderful people, Joe. I'm crazy about them. And I'm going to treat my own parents with . . . with

a certain dignity. My God, the things they said to
me—they seared my soul forever—

*And without drawing a breath she hums a few bars of a
popular song. She has a book before her eyes—but her
eyes are closed.*

MAN: Joseph Brennan was the only child of Mick and
Nora Brennan. Because of his asthma, Mick Brennan
has not had a job for over twenty years. He receives un-
employment benefit and this is supplemented by the
earnings of his wife, who works as a charwoman from
8:00 A.M. until 8:00 P.M., six days a week, for 2/6d
an hour. In a good week her wages come to around
£9/0/od. She has £113/10/6d in post-office savings
and £3/5/7d in an ornate tea caddy in the kitchen.
She is a quiet woman, and all her dreams and love
and hope and delight were centered unashamedly in
Joe.

   Mick Brennan—or Mick the Moocher, as he is known
in Ballymore—is keenly interested in horses, grey-
hounds, ferrets, and pigeons. He spends most of his day
at the greyhound track. To his friends he talked a lot
about Joe, always referring to him in a casual, dis-
paraging way as The Lad.

   Nora Brennan has no hobbies.

WOMAN: Margaret Enright was the daughter of Walter
and Beth Enright. Walter is a dentist. When he married, he was the only dentist in Ballymore. Now there
are three; and his practice is the smallest. As a young

man he was interested in books and travel and music. Now, after his work, he sits at home, and drinks, and reads thrillers. Beth, his wife, has been under Doctor Watson's care for seventeen years, ever since the death of her infant son. She gave birth to twins—Margaret and Peter—and five days after the birth Peter was discovered in his cot, smothered by a pillow. She never fully recovered from this. In her good days she is carefree—almost reckless. In her bad days she wears dark glasses and lies in bed. Walter looks after her constantly.

MAG *is drowsy with the heat. Her head is propped against her case. Through slitted eyes she surveys the scene below in Ballymore. She is addressing* JOE *but knows that he is not listening to her.*

MAG: I can see the boarders out on the tennis courts. They should be studying. And there's a funeral going up High Street; nine cars, and a petrol lorry, and an ambulance. Maybe the deceased was run over by the petrol lorry—the father of a large family—and the driver is paying his respects and crying his eyes out. If he doesn't stop blubbering, he'll run over someone else. And the widow is in the ambulance, all in plaster, crippled for life. (*She tries out a mime of this—both arms and legs cast in awkward shapes.*) And the children are going to be farmed out to cruel aunts with squints and mustaches. Sister Michael has a beard. Joan O'Hara says she shaves with a cut-throat every first Friday and uses an after-shave lotion called Virility.

God, nuns are screams if you don't take them seriously. I think I'd rather be a widow than a widower; but I'd rather be a bachelor than a spinster. And I'd rather be deaf than dumb; but I'd rather be dumb than blind. And if I had to choose between lung cancer, a coronary, and multiple sclerosis, I'd take the coronary. Papa's family all died of coronaries, long before they were commonplace. (*She sits up to tell the following piece of family history.*) He had a sister, Nan, who used to sing at the parochial concert every Christmas; and one year, when she was singing *Jerusalem*—you know, just before the chorus, when the piano is panting Huh-huh-huh-huh-huh-huh, she opened her mouth and dropped like a log . . .

Joe, d'you think (*quoting something she has read*) my legs have got thick, my body gross, my facial expression passive to dull, and my eyes lack-luster? I hope it's a boy, and that it'll be like you—with a great big bursting brain. Or maybe it'll be twins—like me. I wonder what Peter would have been like? Sometimes when she's very ill Mother calls me Peter. If it were going to be twins I'd rather have a boy and a girl than two boys or two girls; but if it were going to be triplets I'd rather have two boys and a girl or two girls and a boy than three boys or three girls. (*Very wisely and directed to* JOE) And I have a feeling it's going to be premature.

JOE *is alerted. His eyes move away from his book, but his head does not move.*

MAG: Mothers have intuitions about these things. We were premature. Five weeks. Very tricky.

JOE: Tricky?

MAG: Caesarean, as a matter of fact.

JOE *has never heard the term.*

JOE: (*Too casually*) That—sure—sure that's—so was I too.

MAG: (*Delighted*) Were you? Isn't that marvelous! We really have everything in common! Oh, Joe, wait till you hear: I was doing my hair this morning, and d'you know what I found in the comb? A gray hair! I'm old! Two months pregnant and I'm as gray as a badger! Isn't it a scream! I think a young face and silver hair is more attractive than an old face and black hair. But if I had to choose between a young face and black hair and an old face and silver hair I think I'd prefer the young face. (*Gently*) You have a young face. You're only a boy. You're only a baby really. I'll have two babies to take care of. (*She touches his shoe.*) Joe, we'll be happy, Joe, won't we? It's such a beautiful morning. So still. I think this is the most important moment in my life. And I think (*she laughs with embarrassment*) I think sometimes that happiness, real happiness, was never discovered until we discovered it. Isn't that silly? And I want to share it with everyone—everywhere.

JOE: Stupid.

MAG: What?

JOE: A fat lot you have to give.

MAG: I didn't say give!

JOE: You did!

MAG: I did not!

JOE: I heard you!

MAG: Liar! I said "share"!

JOE: Share what?

MAG: You wouldn't understand!

JOE: Understand what?

MAG *has lost the thread of the argument.*

MAG: Anything! 'Cos you're just a selfish, cold, horrible, priggish, conceited donkey! Stuck in your old books as if they were the most important thing in the world; and your—your—your intended waiting like a dog for you to toss her a kind word!

JOE: I only asked.

MAG: You hate me—that's it—you're going to marry me just to crush me! I've heard of men like you—sadicists! I've read about them in books! But I never thought for a second—

She breaks off suddenly and claps her stomach in terrified agony. At the same time she is pleasantly aware of JOE's *mounting panic.*

MAG: Oh, my God—!

JOE: What?

MAG: Ooooooooooh—!

JOE: What—what—what is it, Maggie?

MAG: Joe—!

JOE: Mag, are you sick? Are you sick, Mag?

MAG: (*Formally*)   Labor has commenced.

JOE: (*In panic*)   Sweet God! How d'you know? What's happening? I'll get help! Don't move! Doctor Watson warned you to stop cycling! How d'you feel? I'll carry you. Don't move—don't move!

In total consternation he searches her face, noting every flicker of every feature. She is gratified at his anxiety. She acts the brave sufferer.

MAG: I . . . think—

JOE: Don't talk! Don't move! Where did you leave your bike?

MAG: Stay with me, Joe, please. Hold my hand.

JOE: God, this is fierce! On top of a bloody hill! You're all right, Mag, aren't you? Aren't you all right?

She gives him a brave smile.

MAG: Dear Joe. I'm fine, thank you, Joe.

JOE: What's happening? Tell me.

MAG: Nothing to be alarmed about. False pains.

JOE: False . . . ?

MAG: (*Cheerily*) Gone again. For the time being.

JOE: They'll be back?

MAG: Oh, yes. But maybe not for a month.

JOE: God, I'm not worth tuppence.

MAG: I'm sorry for calling you names.

JOE: Maybe you should go home, Mag, eh?

MAG: I'm fine. Really. Go on with your work.

JOE: God, I don't know.

MAG: (*Smiling reassuringly*) Please. I'll just rest.

JOE *gropes for something tender to say. But he is too embarrassed.*

JOE: Maggie, I'll . . . I'll try . . . I'll try to be—

MAG: (*A revelation*) I know now!

JOE: Huh?

MAG: No breakfast!

JOE: What are you—?

MAG: Hunger pangs! That's what it was! I'm ravenous!

JOE: Hunger—?

MAG: I could eat the side of a horse!

JOE: But you said you didn't care—?

MAG: Don't be always quoting what I said. There's nothing as detestable as being quoted. I change my mind every two minutes. Or would you rather it was labor?

JOE: (*Totally baffled*) I . . . I . . . (*Resolutely*) I'm going to work.

He begins to study again. MAG *opens her case and takes out a packet of sandwiches.*

MAG: All the same, if I eat now, I'll have nothing left for later. I'll do with two small sandwiches. Three. (*Eats vigorously.*) My big regret now is that I dropped domestic science in junior. Can't even remember how to make rock buns. And poor old Dorothy Quilty was so sweet to us all. Did I ever tell you what happened to her, Joe? (*She waits for a reply, gets none, and goes on anyhow.*) She was from Dublin. And one afternoon, during the Christmas holidays, she went to the pictures. And this man sat in the seat beside her—gospel truth—Joan O'Hara heard it from a cousin of hers who's a guard in Dundalk. And anyhow during the film this fellow gave her an injection in the arm. Of course no one saw him. And when she passed out he carried her out to the street, and his accomplice was waiting there in a car, and they drove off with her. (*Waits again for* JOE's *reaction. Then goes on.*) And four days later she was found in the Wicklow mountains—up a sycamore tree.

JOE *turns round slowly to face her.*

JOE: What d'you mean—up a sycamore tree?

MAG: Hiding.

JOE: Hiding what?

MAG: Herself. In the leaves.

JOE: (*Deliberately*) You really are crazy.

MAG: She was hiding in the leaves, stupid, because they had taken her clothes away—that's the way. And for your knowledge and information, she had to give up teaching after that experience. Nervous . . . Nervosity; that's what the doctor said she had. And she's now a stitcher in a Belfast shirt factory—of all girls.

JOE: For a woman that's going to be married in four weeks' time—

MAG: Three.

JOE: Honest to God, the stories that you come out with —juvenile, that's the only word for them. And I'm trying to work at integration. So will you shut up?

MAG: (*With dignity*) I will. I certainly will. And the next time I break breath with you, you'll be a chastened man.

Brief pause.

MAG: But before I go silent for the rest of the day, there's something I want to get clear between us, Joseph Brennan. (*Pause.*) Joe.

JOE: What?

MAG: You never proposed to me.

JOE: Huh?

MAG: You haven't *asked* me to marry you.

JOE: What are you raving about?

MAG: Propose to me.

JOE: God!

MAG: Now.

JOE: You really are—!

MAG: Ask me.

JOE: Will-you-marry-me. Now!

MAG: Thank you, Joseph. I will.

He goes back to his books.

JOE: Bats! Raving bloody bats!

MAG: The children will want to know. Especially the girls. And I'll tell them it was a beautiful morning in June, a Saturday, four days before the exams began, on top of Ardnageeha, the Hill of the Wind. And everything was still. And their father said, "Maggie," very shyly, "Maggie Enright, will you make me the proudest and happiest man in the whole world? Will you be my spouse?" And I said, "Joe"—nothing more. And I think that was the most important moment in my life.

She looks at JOE, *sees him engrossed in his work, has a sudden stab of anxiety and grabs a book.*

MAG: I really am scootrified this time! Integration—that's on my course, too—I think. What in the name of God does it mean?

She buries her head in her hands and studies furiously.

MAN: It is estimated that Joe Brennan and Maggie Enright came down from the top of Ardnageeha around two o'clock that afternoon. They were seen walking hand-in-hand along the Mill Road at about ten past two; and ten minutes later they were seen going in the direction of Lough Gorm, which lies to the east of Ballymore. Both were on foot. Joe was wheeling Maggie's bicycle. The recorded temperature at 3:00 P.M. on that Saturday afternoon, June 4, 1966, was 77 degrees. And there was no wind.

WOMAN: Lough Gorm is three miles long and half a mile broad, and there are forty-nine islands of various sizes scattered over it. There are seven boats on the lake. And on that afternoon two of them were out. Philip Moran and Joan O'Hara were out in Mr.

O'Hara's boat. They went out at noon and returned at
1:30. The other boat was William Anthony Clerkin's,
an accountant in the local bank. He fished from eleven
that morning until two that afternoon. Then he pulled
in on the south shore, beside the old lime kiln, and
went home for his lunch. He left the oars and rowlocks
lying in the boat. When he returned an hour and
twenty minutes later, the boat was gone; and a girl's
bicycle was lying at the edge of the water.

MAG: I'll tell you a tip. (*Pause.*) Joe. (*Pause.*) D'you
want to know a clever trick I have, Joe? In all exams
the smart thing to do is to write down everything you
know—no matter what the question is. Les oiseaux qui
en sont dehors désespèrent d'y entrer; et d'un pareil
soin en sortir, ceux qui sont au-dedans; if the moving
line is at right angles to the plane figure, the prism is
a right prism; in 1586 Sir Philip Sidney met his death
at Zutphen from a wound in the nether regions of his
body; the volume of a cone is $\frac{1}{3}\pi$ dh multiplied by—
my God, and that's the one thing I know! Shakespeare,
the Bard of Avon, besides writing thirty-four extant
plays, was married to a woman eight years his senior,
and was the father of twins. Like Papa. As flies to
wanton boys are we to the gods; they kill us for their
sport. Sister Pascal says that you always know Prot-
estants by their yellow faces and Catholics by their
dirty fingernails. (*She rises, moves away from* JOE, *who
is lost in his books, and stands at the edge of the hill-
top. She looks down over the town.*) Nuns are screams—
if you don't take them seriously . . . I don't know what

things I take seriously . . . Never books or school or things like that . . . Maybe God sometimes, when I'm in trouble . . . and Papa . . . and being a good wife to you . . . It's so quiet, with the whole world before me . . . Joe (*She turns to face him*) Joe, you'll have to talk a lot more to me, Joe. I don't care if it's not sensible talk; it's just that—you know—I feel lonely at times . . . Of course I'll have Joan; she'll visit us; Phil and herself. And you'll like her better when you get to know her. All that's wrong with her is that she's not mature yet; and she can be cruel at times . . .

After we're married we'll have lots of laughs to- gether, Joe, won't we? We'll laugh a lot, won't we? (*She begins to cry inaudibly.*) Joe, I'm nervous; I'm frightened, Joe; I'm terrified . . .

MAN: At 6:20 William Anthony Clerkin reported to Sergeant Finlay that his boat had been stolen. The Sergeant and Mr. Clerkin returned to Lough Gorm and walked around a portion of the south shore. They sighted the upturned boat floating about fifty yards west of the biggest island, Oilean Na Gcrann.

WOMAN: As a result of inquiries, the Sergeant learned that the bicycle belonged to Margaret Mary Enright. He phoned the Enright home and discovered that the girl had left there early in the morning. He then called at the Brennan home and Mr. Brennan informed him that he had not seen his son all day.

MAG: I will tell my secrets to my baby.

MAN: It was then 7:45 P.M.

WOMAN: At 8:10 a search party of twenty-three local men set out to search the forty-nine islands.

MAG *has another twinge of conscience: she plunges into her book again.*

MAG: (*Reads*) LP, MQ, and NR are ordinates perpendicular to the axis OX such that LP=8″, MQ=7″, and NR=4″. Find the lengths of the ordinates at the midpoints of LM and MN of the circular arc through P, Q, and R, and by means of Simpson's rule and the five ordinates estimate . . . (*Her concentration fails.*) Everything's so still. That's what I love. At a time like this, if I close my eyes and scarcely breathe, I sometimes have very important philosophic thoughts—about existence and life and et cetera. That's what people mean when they talk of a woman's intuitions. Every woman has intuitions but I think that pregnant women have more important intuitions than non-pregnant women. And another thing too: a woman's intuitions are more important while she's pregnant than after she's had her baby. So when you see a pregnant woman sitting at the fire, knitting, not talking, you can be sure she's having very important philosophic thoughts about things. I wish to God I could knit. Years and years ago in primary school I began a pair of gloves; but the fingers scootrified me and I turned them into ankle socks . . .

I think your father's a highly intellectual man, really;

a born naturalist. And your mother—she's so practical
and so unassuming. That's what I want to be. One of
these days I'm going to stop talking altogether—for
good—and people will say: Didn't Mrs. Joseph Brennan become dignified all of a sudden? Since the baby
arrived, I suppose. I think now, Joe, it's going to be
nineteen days overdue. And in desperation they'll
bring me into the hospital and put me on the tread-
mill—that's a new yoke they have to bring on labor;
Joan told me about it. An aunt of a second cousin of
hers was on it non-stop for thirteen hours. They keep
you climbing up this big wheel that keeps giving away
under you. Just like the slaves in olden times. And
after the baby's born they'll keep it in an oxygen tent
for a fortnight. And when we get it home it'll have
to be fed with an eye dropper every forty-nine minutes and we'll get no sleep at all and— (*Sudden alarm-
ing thought*) My God, you won't get asthma like your
father when you get old, will you?

JOE: . . . equals $2.8 \times t \times p$ all over pv to the power of $1.4 \times$
v . . .

MAG: Even if you do, I'll rub your chest with menthol
and give you the kiss of life.

JOE: Shhhhhh.

*She watches him for a moment in silence. He is unaware
of her existence.*

MAG: There's something I want to tell you, Joe, and there's something I want to ask you as well. And I think I'll ask you the thing I want to ask you before I tell you the thing I want to tell you. (*Pause.*) Joe.

JOE: (*Very irritable*) What-what-what?

MAG: My parents sleep in separate rooms. Do yours?

JOE: In our house there are two bedrooms. I'm in one of them.

MAG: And do they—have a single bed or a double bed?

JOE: Double. Satisfied, Nosy?

MAG: (*Fully gratified*) I knew that was a real marriage. That's what I want. Like your parents. Joe, there's something I want to try to explain to you, too.

JOE: Look—five minutes more—that's all I ask.

He does not listen to her.

MAG: I look at Papa and Mother, and Mr. and Mrs. O'Hara, and all the other parents and I think—I think —none of them knows what being in love really is. And that's why I think we're different. God, doesn't that sound stupid when you say it! But that's the way I feel, Joe. At this moment—here—now—I'm crazy about you— and mad and reckless, so that I want to shout to the

whole town: I love Joe Brennan! I'm mad about him!
I'd do anything for him! D'you hear me, Mother
Dolores? I love him so much—so much—that I want to
—to become him! Isn't that stupid? And when I look
around me—at Papa and Mother and the O'Haras—
I think: by God we'll never become like that, because
—don't laugh at me, Joe—because I think we're unique!
Is that how you feel, too?

JOE *flings his book from him in exasperation. Speaks
very articulately.*

JOE: You-are-a-bloody-pain-in-the-neck! (*Quickly*) You
haven't shut up for five consecutive minutes since we
got here! You have done no work yourself and you
have wasted my morning, too! And if anyone should
be working, it's you, because you haven't a clue about
anything! In fact, you're the stupidest person I ever
met!

MAG: Stewbag!

JOE: Sticks and stones—go ahead!

MAG: And you can't kick a football the length of yourself!

JOE: What has that got to do with it?

MAG: That's what everybody calls you 'cos that's all you
can do is stew—stew—stew!

JOE: Born stupid.

MAG: (*Crying*) Stewbag! Stewbag!

JOE: Bawl away. Bawl your head off. But if you think I'm going to waste my life in Skinny Skeehan's smelly office, that's where you're mistaken. You trapped me into marrying you—that's all right—I'll marry you. But I'll lead my own life. And somehow—somehow I'll get a degree and be a maths teacher. And nobody, neither you nor your precious baby nor anyone else, is going to stop me! So put that in your pipe and smoke it!

He opens his book and pretends to work: but he is too agitated. MAG *covers her face and cries.*

MAN: The search was continued without interruption for three days. An SOS was broadcast, and ports and airports were watched. It was reported to the police that a young couple answering to the description were seen in Liverpool and later in the Waterford area. But an investigation proved both reports to be false. Margaret Mary Enright and Joseph Michael Brennan had disappeared.

WOMAN: On Wednesday, June 8, the search was called off.

Curtain

EPISODE 2

The sun is warmer because it is early afternoon. JOE
and MAG *have had their lunch: papers and paper cups
are lying around.*

MAG *is stretched out on the ground, her head pillowed
on her case; the essense of sloth. Her eyes are closed.*

JOE *is working at a calculation with total concentration.*

WOMAN: The months of June and July 1966 were the
warmest and driest Ballymore has had since records
have been kept. The water supply to the town had to
be cut off for three hours each morning because the
level of Lough Gorm dropped by almost two feet.

MAN: Beth Enright, Margaret's mother, spent the greater
portion of these months in the County Psychiatric
Clinic. She was visited daily by Walter, her husband,
and on two occasions by Nora Brennan, Joseph's
mother, who brought her grapes and magazines.

JOE *has finished his calculation. He closes his books with
a satisfied flourish.*

JOE: Maths done! They can do their damndest now—
I'm ready for them! I'll tell you something, Mag: you
know when you're sitting in the exam hall and the
papers have just been given out and your eye runs
down the questions? Well, those are the happiest mo-
ments in my life. There's always that tiny uncertainty
that maybe this time they'll come up with something
that's going to throw you; but that only adds to the
thrill because you know in your heart you're . . . in-
vincible. (*He begins to put his books away: because
he is on top of his work, he is in an expansive mood.*)
I didn't tell you; I met old Skinny Skeehan: "I'll start
you in my office, lad, as soon as your exams are over.
On your mother's account I hope you're a good time-
keeper and that your writing is legible." I never
looked at him right before: his eyelids are purple and
his ears are all hairy. So I just said to him: "Stick your
clerkship up your legal ass and get a lawnmower at
those ears of yours"—like hell. But that's what I should
have said, the hungry get. (*Mentally ticking off*) About
another hour to French and the same at history and
I'll leave the English to tomorrow. Remember I was
telling you how George Simpson got an extern degree
at London University? Well, I wrote to them last night
for a syllabus. Three years; that's all it takes. Joseph
Brennan, Bachelor of Science. Then, by God, the
world's our oyster. You asleep, Mag?

MAG *neither moves nor opens her eyes.*

MAG: No.

JOE: Nothing wrong with you, is there?

MAG: No.

JOE: Are you in bad form or something?

MAG: No.

JOE: Did I do anything, Mag?

MAG: No.

JOE: As long as those false pains don't come back. (*Going on gaily*) Pity we hadn't our togs. Be a great day for a swim, wouldn't it?—if we could swim!

MAG: I trapped you into marrying me—that's what you said.

JOE: Huh?

MAG: That's what you said. Put that in your pipe and smoke it—that's what you said.

JOE: Ah, come on, Mag. You're not huffing still.

MAG: And you meant it, too.

JOE: But you ate your lunch and all. You ate more than I did.

MAG: There was hate in your eyes.

JOE: I'm sorry.

MAG: It's no good.

Pause. Then JOE *decides to win her round by clowning.*

JOE: Mag—

MAG: I'm not looking.

JOE: MAG—

MAG: No.

JOE: Who's this, Mag?

MAG: I'm going asleep.

JOE: (*In mincing voice*) "Tweeny—Tweeny—Tweeny— Tweeny! Come on, Tweeny girl. Atta girl. Come on. Come on."

MAG: That's not one bit like Mr. O'Hara.

JOE: (*In excessive nasal tones*) "Good example is something we should all practice, my dear people. Put one bad apple into a barrel of good apples, and all the good apples become corrupt."

MAG: I'm not listening.

JOE: "But put one good apple into a barrel of bad apples, and then—and then—"

MAG: You're not one bit funny.

JOE: "—and then" (*rapidly*) "devotions this evening at six o'clock in the name of the father son holy ghost."

MAG: (*In matching tone*) Ha-men.

JOE: (*East London*) "So sorry, Joseph, but my Phil 'e's not at 'ome at present."

MAG *suddenly giggles.*

"'E's out on 'is bi-cycle on one of 'is solitary nature rambles."

MAG *sits up. She laughs out loud.*

"Like 'is poor dad used to. I'll tell 'im you called. Bye-bye."

MAG: "Ta-ta."

JOE: "Ta-ta."

MAG: No. "Ta-ta for now."

JOE: "Ta-ta for now."

MAG: "Call again soon, Joseph."

JOE: "I like my Phil to 'ave chum boys."

They both howl with spontaneous, helpless laughter. When they try to speak, they cannot finish.

MAG: Sister Pascal—

JOE: Wha—

MAG: Sister Pascal—

JOE: —is a rascal!

MAG: She says that for every five minutes you laugh, you—

JOE: You what—?

MAG: —you cry for ten!

This seems the crowning absurdity. They roll on the ground.

JOE: Oooooooh . . . !

MAG: God, I'm sore!

JOE: Cruel!

MAG: We'll cry for weeks!

JOE: Nuns—bloody nuts!

MAG: Give me a handkerchief.

*He throws her one. She wipes her eyes. They sober up—
and wonder what set them off. She lights a cigarette.*

JOE: What started that?

MAG: I don't know.

JOE: Give me (*handkerchief*). Oh, my God.

MAG: Leave you weak.

JOE: This whole town's nuts.

MAG *is stretched out under the sun again. A wistful mood
creeps over them now that the laughter is forgotten.*

MAG: D'you think they'll get married?

JOE: Who?

MAG: Joan and Philip.

JOE: How would I know? They're only seventeen.

MAG: They say they're both going to be architects.

JOE: How long does that take?

MAG: Seven years. Maybe then.

JOE *busies himself with gathering up the remains of the lunch.*

JOE: Maybe then what?

MAG: Maybe then they'll marry, after they qualify.

JOE: Maybe. Who cares.

MAG: I don't.

JOE: Neither do I.

MAG: Why talk about them then?

JOE: You mentioned them first.

MAG: You did. You imitated Mr. O'Hara and Phil's mother.

JOE: Maggie, I did not mention Joan O'Hara's name. As a matter of fact, I can't stick the girl.

MAG: Sister Pascal was right.

JOE: What about?

MAG: We *will* cry for twice the length.

JOE: For God's sake, woman!

He heads off down the far side of the hill to get rid of the old papers he has gathered.

MAG: (*Quickly*) Where are you going?

JOE: I am going to dispose of this stuff—if I have your permission.

MAG: You don't have to have my permission for anything. And I don't have to have yours either. 'Cos I'm not married to you yet, Mr. Brennan, in case you have forgotten.

JOE: No, I haven't forgotten.

He disappears. She calls after him.

MAG: Well, just in case you should! (*She settles back and closes her eyes resolutely.*)

MAN: On Tuesday, June 21, a local boy was driving his father's cows down to the edge of Lough Gorm for a drink when he saw what he described as "bundles of clothes" floating just off the north shore. He ran home and told his mother.

WOMAN: The police were informed, and Sergeant Finlay

accompanied by two constables went to investigate. The "bundles" were the bodies of Mary Margaret Enright and Joseph Michael Brennan. They were floating, fully clothed, face down, in twenty-seven inches of water.

MAN: A post-mortem was held in the parochial hall at 7:00 P.M. that evening.

JOE *has returned. He speaks with a dignified sincerity.*

JOE: Mag, there is something I never told you. And since you are going to be my wife, I don't want there to be any secrets between us. I have a post-office book. I have had it since I was ten. And there is £23/15/0d. in it now. I intend spending that money on a new suit, new shoes, and an electric razor. And I'm mentioning this to you now in case you suspect I have other hidden resources. I haven't. (*He cannot maintain this tone. He continues naturally.*) And I was working out our finances. The rent of the flat's two-ten. That'll leave us with about four-ten. And if I could get some private pupils, that would bring in another—say—thirty bob. We can manage fine on that, can't we? I mean, I can. What about you? (*Looks down at her.*) Mag? You asleep, Mag? How the hell can you sleep when you have no work done? Maggie . . . ? (*He kneels beside her and looks into her face. He gently puts her hair away from her eyes. He straightens up as he remembers the word Caesarean.*) Dictionary . . . (*He gets his own dictionary and searches for the word.*) Cadet . . .

cadge . . . Caesar . . . Caesarean, pertaining to Caesar or the Caesars—section—an operation by which the walls of the stomach are cut open and . . . (*Shocked and frightened*) . . . Cripes! (*Reads*) As with Julius— oh, my God! If I see you on that bike again I'll break your bloody neck! As with Julius—good God! Maggie, are you all right, Maggie? O God, that's wild, wild! Sleep, Mag; that's bound to be good for you. (*He lifts her blazer and spreads it over her.*) There. God almighty! Cut open. (*Takes the blazer off.*) Maybe you'll be too warm. God, I'd sit ten exams every day sooner than this! Don't say a word, Maggie; just sleep and rest! That twenty-three pound fifteen—it's for you, Maggie. And I want you to to—to squander it just as you wish: fur coats, dresses, perfumes, make-up, all that stuff—anything in the world you want—don't even tell me what you spend it on; I don't want to know. It's yours. And curtains for the window—whatever you like. God, Mag, I never thought for a minute it was that sort of thing! (*He looks closely at her.*) Mag . . . (*Whispers*) Mag, I'm not half good enough for you. I'm jealous and mean and spiteful and cruel. But I'll try to be tender to you and good to you; and that won't be hard because even when I'm not with you— just when I think of you—I go all sort of silly and I say to myself over and over again: *I'm crazy about Maggie Enright;* and so I am—crazy about you. You're a thousand times too good for me. But I'll try to be good to you; honest to God, I'll try. (*He kisses her hand and replaces it carefully across her body. Then with sudden venom*) Those Caesars were all gets! (*He takes*

an apple from one of the lunch bags, gets out his
penknife, and peels it. As he does, he talks to MAG
even though he knows she is asleep.) I hope it's a girl,
like you; with blond hair like yours. 'Cos if it's a boy it'll
be a bloody hash, like me. And every night when I
come home from Skeehan's office I'll teach her maths
and she'll grow up to be a prodigy. I saw a program on
TV once about an American professor who spoke to
his year-old daughter in her cot in four different lan-
guages for an hour every day; and when the child began to talk she could converse in German, French,
Spanish, and Italian. Imagine if my aul fella looked
down into our wee girl's cot and she shouted up to
him: "Buenos dias!" Cripes, he'd think she was giving
him a tip for a horse! I hope to God it's a girl. But if
it's twins I'd rather have two boys or two girls than
. . . (*He glances shyly at* MAGGIE *and tails off sheep-*
ishly when he realizes he has fallen into her speech pat-
tern.) . . . D'you hear me? That's the way married
people go. They even begin to look alike. Wonder is
old Skinny Skeehan married? I bet she looks like a
gatepost . . . Your father, Mag, my God he's such a
fine man. And your mother—I mean she's such a fine
woman. I remember—oh, I was only a boy at the time
—I remember seeing them walking together out the
Dublin Road; and I thought they were so—you know
—so dignified-looking. I'd like to be like him. God,
such a fine man. And so friendly to everyone. You're
lucky to have parents like that . . .

My aul fella—lifting the dole on a Friday—that's
what he lives for. She laughs and calls him her man

Friday; but I don't know how she can laugh at it.
And to listen to him talking—cripes, you'd think he
was bloody Solomon. How he can sit on his backside
and watch her go out every morning with her apron
wrapped in a newspaper under her arm—honest to
God, I don't know how he does it. I said it to her once,
you know; called him a loafer or something. And you
should have seen her face! I thought she was going to
hit me! "Don't you ever—ever—say the likes of that
again. You'll never be half the man he is." Loyalty,
I suppose; 'cos when you're that age, you hardly—
you know—really love your husband or wife any more
. . . Did I ever tell you what he does when there's no
racing? He has this tin trunk under his bed; he keeps
all my old school reports in it. And he sits up there in
the cold and takes out the trunk and pores over all
those old papers—term reports and all, away back to
my primary-school days! Real nut! I know damn well
when he's at it 'cos I can hear the noise of the trunk
on the lino. And once when I went into the room he
tried to stuff all the papers out of sight. Strange, too,
isn't it . . . You know, we never speak at all, except
maybe "Is the tea ready?" or "Bring in some coal"
. . . Sitting up there in that freezing attic, going over
my old marks . . .

Maybe when I'm older, maybe we'll go to football
matches together, like Peadar Donnelly and his aul
fella . . . I don't like football matches, but he does; and
we shouldn't have to speak to each other—except going
and coming back . . . Three years is no length for a
degree. And I think myself I'd be a good teacher.

MAG *speaks but does not move or open her eyes. Her voice is sleepy.*

MAG: What time is it?

JOE: Quarter to two.

MAG: Call me at half past, will you? I have a bit of revision to do.

JOE: A bit?! You've done nothing!

MAG *has dropped off again.*

JOE: Mag!

MAG: Mm?

JOE: That's all right! You go ahead and sleep! But I'm telling you: if I die of a heart attack and leave you with a dozen kids, you'll be damned sorry you haven't your GCE ordinary levels!

She sits up and stares at him. He goes on defiantly.

I'm just being practical. Nowadays you're fit for nothing unless you have an education. And you needn't stare at me like that: any qualification is better than nothing. You'll always get some sort of a job. Hennigan that teaches us PT—that's all he has—is GCE. And I'm telling you: I wouldn't give a shilling for your chances at the moment!

MAG: And the children?

JOE: What children?

MAG: Who's going to look after the dozen children when I'm up at Saint Kevin's teaching physical jerks?

JOE: Oh, you're very smart.

MAG: And where, may I ask, did the round dozen come from all of a sudden?

JOE: Cut it out, will you? You know what I meant.

MAG: Indeed I do. And if you think I'm going to spend my days like big Bridie Brogan—

JOE: Who's she supposed to be?

MAG: She's married to a second cousin once removed of Joan O'Hara's—

JOE: God, I might have known! If there's anyone I hate—

MAG: —and after her third baby the doctor told her she'd die if she had any more; but her husband was an Irish brute and she had a fourth baby—

JOE: And she died.

MAG: She didn't die, smartie. But she lost her sight. And then she had a fifth baby—

JOE: And she died.

MAG: —and she went deaf. And she couldn't walk after the sixth. And after the seventh she had to get all her teeth out—

JOE: Sounds like the Rose of Tralee.

MAG: And by the time she had ten—

JOE: Her husband died laughing at her.

MAG: —she developed pernicious micropia.

JOE: Pernicious what?

MAG: I'm not in the habit of repeating myself. Anyhow, she's thirty-three now and—

JOE: You made that word up.

MAG: I did not.

JOE: You did, Maggie.

MAG: I did not.

JOE: Say it again, then.

MAG: I told you—I'm not in—

JOE: Pernicious what?

MAG: You're too ignorant to have heard of it. My father came across frequent cases of it. I don't suppose your parents ever heard of it.

As soon as she has said this, she regrets it. But she cannot retract now. JOE's *banter is suddenly ended. He is quietly furious.*

JOE: Just what do you mean by that?

MAG: What I say.

JOE: I said: what do you mean by that remark?

MAG: You heard me.

JOE: You insulted my parents—deliberately.

MAG: I was talking about a disease.

JOE: You think they're nobody, don't you?

MAG: You were mocking me.

JOE: And you think your parents are somebody, don't you?

MAG *picks a book, opens it at random, turns her back to him, and begins to read.*

MAG: I have revision to do.

JOE: Well, let me tell you, madam, that my father may be temporarily unemployed, but he pays his bills; and *my* mother may be a charwoman but she isn't running out to the mental hospital for treatment every couple of months. And if you think the Brennans aren't swanky enough for you, then by God you shouldn't be in such a hurry to marry one of them!

As soon as he has said this, he regrets it. But he cannot retract now.

You dragged that out of me. But it happens to be the truth. And it's better that it should come out now than *after* we're married. At least we know where we stand . . . (*His anger is dead.*) Margaret? . . . Maggie? . . . (*Stiff again*) Well, it was you that started it. And if you're going into another of your huffs, I swear to you I'm not going to be the first to speak this time.

He picks a book, opens it at random, turns his back to her, and begins to read.

WOMAN: At the post-mortem on the evening of June 21 evidence of identification was given by Walter Enright. He said that the body recovered from Lough Gorm was the body of his daughter, Margaret Mary Enright.

MAN: Michael Brennan identified the male body as that of his son, Joseph Michael Brennan.

WOMAN: Doctor Watson said that he had examined the
bodies of both the deceased. There were no marks of
violence on either, he said. And in his opinion—which,
he submitted, was given after a hasty examination—
death in both cases was due to asphyxiation.

MAN: Mr. Skeehan, the coroner, asked was there any
evidence as to how both deceased fell into the water.
Sergeant Finlay replied that there was no evidence.

WOMAN: A verdict in accordance with the medical evidence was returned. Mr. Skeehan and Sergeant Finlay expressed their grief and the grief of the community to the parents. And it was agreed that the
inquest should be held as soon as possible because the
coroner took his annual vacation in the month of
July.

JOE *looks up from his book and surveys the countryside
with studied intelligence. When he speaks he tries to
sound as matter-of-fact as possible—as if he were continu-
ing a conversation: but his voice is strained.*

JOE: We're about 450 feet above sea level here; isn't that
interesting? (*Pause.*) And all that area out there was
covered with fir trees once. (*Pause.*) Willie O'Rourke
did a survey of the whole area for his geography
practical last term and he found out all sorts of fascinat-
ing things. (*Pause.*) The average rainfall in Ballymore is 17.4 percent above the county average and
23.9 percent above the national average. (*Pause.*)
That's because we get a lot of rain here. (*Quoting*)

And the moist climate determines the type and extent of our husbandry: we are low in milk cattle and high in mountain sheep. (*Pause.*) And since a ring of hills cuts us off from other community centers we are traditionally inclined to be independent and self-supporting—or so he claims. (*Pause.*) It's an interesting hypothesis. (*Pause.*) Busy?

No answer.

(*Formally*) I'm sorry for losing my temper. (*Opens another book.*) If you have anything to say to me, you'll find me here.

No answer. He looks at her.

You crying? . . . Mag? . . .

Still no answer. He rises and stands behind her.

What the hell are you crying about, Mag? . . . Mag . . .

He goes in front of her. She turns her back to him.

I said I'm sorry. What more can I do . . . ? (*Pause.*) It's going to be just great if you're going to spend your life weeping all the time!

He casts around wretchedly for something to entertain her. Decides on mimicry.

(*As* MRS. MORAN) "Well, I mean to say—smoking at 'is age! I just says to 'im, 'Phil,' I says, 'if your poor daddy was alive, 'e'd be so vexed,' I says. 'Ta-ta for now, Joe. Ta-ta for now.'"

No response from MAG.

(*As* KERRIGAN) "What about that for a bit of beef, eh? Bang. Best flat in town, lad. I could have let it a dozen times over. Bang. Bang. Bang."

No response.

Mag . . . Mag, is it true that in bed at night the nuns wear their bloomers over their heads to keep them warm?

No response.

JOE!
   (*Sings*)

So I gave her kisses one, kisses one;
So I gave her kisses one, kisses one;
So I gave her kisses one—now the fun has just begun
So I settled down to give her kisses more.
(*Says*) I'd be great on TV, wouldn't I?

No response.

When Father Kelly sent for me last Friday fortnight, I knew I was done for, and I pretended I was so frightened I had a stammer—did I tell you that part of it?

(*Pompous*) You know, of course, Brennan, that we are going to expel you.

(*Abject*) Yes, F-f-f-father.

(*Pompous*) Because of your mother's pleadings on your behalf, however, we have decided to allow you to return to sit for your examinations. But in the meantime I must insist that you remove all your belongings from the college and that you don't set foot within the grounds until the morning of the first examination.

(*Abject*) T-t-t-thank you, Father.

(*Pompous*) I will not talk again about the dishonor you have brought to your school, your family, and yourself. And I trust you have made your peace with God. Goodbye, Brennan.

(*Abject*) Goodbye, Father.

(*Pompous*) Incidentally, Brennan, when did you develop the stammer?

(*Abject*) W-w-w-when Maggie told me she was in trouble, Father.

MAG *began chuckling silently—and unnoticed by* JOE—*at the beginning of this interview. Now she can contain her laughter no longer. At the last line she screams her delight and throws herself at him, and they roll on the ground.*

MAG: God forgive you!

JOE: Stop! Stop! God's truth—

MAG: God forgive you! Mocking's catching!

JOE: Come on—quit the fooling.

MAG: I'll give a stammer.

She tosses his hair and tickles him.

JOE: Mag—please—sorry—please—oooooh—

MAG: I'll stammer you—

JOE: You're hurting my—

MAG: That'll teach you!

JOE: You've ripped off a button—

MAG: You're a right-looking sketch!

Exhausted after the wrestling, they sit staring at one another. Suddenly he throws his arms around her and kisses her. As he does:

MAN: On Saturday, June 25, at 11:00 A.M. an inquest was held.

WOMAN: After various witnesses had given evidence about the movements of the deceased on the morning of Saturday, June 4, Doctor Watson said that the state pathologist's report bore out his initial opinion—that death was due to asphyxiation as a result of drowning.

MAN: There was no evidence as to how the deceased got into the water. William Anthony Clerkin's boat was perfectly sound.

WOMAN: Sergeant Finlay stated that the temperature on that afternoon was 77 degrees. And there was no wind.

MAN: An open verdict was returned.

WOMAN: On the following Sunday, June 5, at 12 noon, a solemn requiem mass was said by Father Kelly, president of Saint Kevin's, and a short panegyric was preached by him. The mass was attended by a large turn-out of the townspeople and also by pupils of the Convent of Mercy and Saint Kevin's.

MAN: The bodies were buried in separate graves in the local cemetery, each in the family plot.

JOE *and* MAG *are now sitting with their arms around one another, looking down over the town. The boisterousness is all over; the mood is calm, content, replete.* MAG *lights a cigarette.*

JOE: This day three weeks.

MAG: Mrs. Joseph Brennan.

JOE: As long as you're not Big Bridie Brogan.

MAG: Who?

JOE: The one who died of pernicious something or other.

MAG: I made that all up.

JOE: Thought you did.

MAG: The flat'll be lovely and cozy at night. But you'll have to stick a bit of cardboard under the table to keep it steady. And all the junk'll have to be thrown into the spare room.

JOE: What junk?

MAG: Your books and things and all that.

JOE: The slide rule cost me 37/6d.—It's staying in the kitchen. And you agreed that the dog sleeps inside.

MAG: When do we get him?

JOE: He's not pupped yet. I was only promised him.

MAG: Maybe he'll be a she.

JOE: It's a dog I'm promised—the pick of the litter.

MAG: We'll call him . . . Austin!

JOE: For God's sake—

MAG: Austin's his name. Or else he sleeps out.

JOE: Never heard of a bull terrier called that.

MAG: And in the daytime he can sit at the door and guard the pram. Look—

JOE: Where?

MAG: The line of boarders.

JOE: What are they up to now?

MAG: Going to the chapel for a visit.

JOE: (*Counting*) 14, 16, 18, 20—

MAG: It seems so remote—so long ago . . .

JOE: —26, 28, 30, 32—

MAG: And at home last week, every time I heard the convent bell, I cried: I felt so lost. I would have given anything to be part of them—to be in the middle of them.

JOE: And three nuns.

MAG: We were so safe . . . we had so much fun . . .

JOE: Mm?

MAG: But now I wouldn't go back for the world. I'm a woman at seventeen, and I wouldn't be a schoolgirl again, not for all the world.

JOE: I suppose I'm a man, too.

MAG: Would you go back?

JOE: Where?

MAG: To Saint Kevin's—to be a schoolboy?

JOE: I never think of things like that.

MAG: But if you could—if you had a chance.

JOE: I like studying, Mag.

MAG: Then you'd prefer to go back.

JOE: No. Not there. I'm finished with all that.

MAG: Then you wouldn't want to go back?

JOE: Not to Saint Kevin's. No.

MAG: Good.

JOE: Know something, Mag?

MAG: Mm?

JOE: I think I should forget about studying and London University and all that.

MAG: If that's what you want.

JOE: It's maybe not what I want. But that's the way things have turned out. A married man with a family has more important things to occupy his mind besides bloody books.

She gives him a brief squeeze. But she has not heard what he has said. Pause.

JOE: Ballymore.

MAG: Home.

JOE: See the sun glinting on the headstones beside the chapel.

MAG: Some day we'll be buried together.

JOE: You're great company.

MAG: I can't wait for the future, Joe.

JOE: What's that supposed to mean?

MAGGIE *suddenly leaps to her feet. Her face is animated, her movements quick and vital, her voice ringing.*

MAG: The past's over! And I hate this waiting time! I want the future to happen—I want to be in it—I want to be in it with you!

JOE: You've got sunstroke.

She throws her belongings into her case.

MAG: Come on, Joe! Let's begin the future now!

Not comprehending, but infected by her mood, he gets to his feet.

JOE: You're nuts.

MAG: Where'll we go? What'll we do? Let's do something crazy!

JOE: Mad as a hatter.

MAG: The lake! We'll dance on every island! We'll stay out all night and sing and shout at the moon!

JOE *does a wolf howl up at the sky.*

Come on, Joe! While the sun's still hot!

JOE: O mad hot sun, thou breath of summer's being!

MAG: Away to the farthest island.

JOE: We've no boat.

MAG: We'll take one.

JOE: And get arrested.

MAG: Coward. Then I'll take one.

JOE: I'll visit you in jail.

MAG: Quick! Quick!

JOE *throws his books into his bag.*

JOE: Hold on there.

MAG: Give me your hand. We'll run down the hill.

JOE: You'll get those pains again.

MAG: Your hand.

JOE: You're not going to run down there.

MAG: Come on! Come on! Come on!

JOE: Have sense, Mag—

She catches his hand and begins to run.

MAG: We're away!

JOE: Easy—easy—

MAG: Wheeeeeeeee—

JOE: Aaaaaaaah—

They run down the hill, hand in hand. At the bottom JOE *takes her bicycle. Their voices fade slowly. Pause. Then:*

MAN: Beth Enright's health has improved greatly. She has not had a relapse for almost seven months. And every evening, if the weather is good, Walter and she go for a walk together out the length of Whelan's Brae.

WOMAN: Mick Brennan never mentions his son's name. After the funeral he took a tin trunk out to the waste ground behind Railway Terrace and burned all the contents. Nora Brennan has had to limit the amount of work she does because her varicose veins turned septic and Doctor Watson ordered her to rest. She now works on afternoons only.

MAN: In the past eight months the population of Ballymore has risen from 13,527 to 13,569.

WOMAN: Life there goes on as usual.

MAN: As if nothing had ever happened.

The MAN *and* WOMAN *close their texts, stand up, and
exit, one left, one right.*

PART TWO

Losers

Cast

ANDY TRACEY
HANNA WILSON/TRACEY
MRS. WILSON
CISSY CASSIDY

The stage is divided into three equal areas: The portion right is the back yard of a working-class terrace house: the center portion is the kitchen/living room; the area left is the bedroom (left and right from the point of view of the audience). There should be no attempt at a realistic division of the stage areas, no dividing walls, no detailed furnishings: frames will indicate doors, etc., etc.

The back yard is suggested by a dustbin and by two high stone walls (one back stage and one right). It is a gray, grimy, gloomy, sunless place.

The kitchen is furnished with a table and a few chairs; and with a disproportionately large horsehair black couch. The couch sits along the imaginary wall between the kitchen and the back yard. There are three doors leading out of the kitchen: one to the yard, one to the scullery (unseen) and one to the hall/stairs (unseen).

The bedroom area is raised on a shallow platform which is approached by two steps (because this room is supposed to be directly above the kitchen). It is furnished with a big iron double bed, a chest of drawers (the "altar"), and a few chairs. Except where indicated, the bedroom will be hidden from the audience by a large draft screen.

TIME: *The present in Ireland.*

When the curtain rises, ANDY TRACEY *is sitting upright and motionless on a kitchen chair in the back yard. He is staring fixedly through a pair of binoculars at the gray stone wall, which is only a few yards from where he is sitting. It becomes obvious that he is watching nothing: there is nothing to watch, and when he becomes aware of the audience, he lowers the glasses slowly, looks at the audience, glances cautiously over his shoulder at the kitchen to make sure that no one in the house overhears him, and then speaks directly and confidentially down to the auditorium.*

He is a man of fifty, a joiner by trade, heavily built. His workmates look on him as a solid, decent, reliable, slightly dull man. Because his mind is simple, direct, unsubtle, he is unaware of the humor in a lot of the things that he says.

ANDY: I'll tell you something: I see damn all through these things. Well, I mean, there's damn all to see in a back yard. Now and again maybe a sparrow or something like that lands on top of the wall there but it's so close it's only a blur. Anyway, most of the time I sit with my eyes closed. And Hanna—she probably knows I do 'cos she's no dozer; but once I come out here—I'll say that for her—she leaves me alone. A gesture I make, and she—you know—she respects it. Maybe because her aul fella used to do the same thing; for that's where I learned the dodge. As a matter of fact, these are his glasses. And this is where he was found dead, the poor bugger, just three years ago, slumped in a chair out here, and him all happed up in his cap and his top coat and his muffle and his woolen gloves. Wait—I'm telling you a lie. Four years ago—aye—that's more like it, 'cos he passed away that January Hanna and me started going, and we won't be married four years until next summer. Not that I knew the man, beyond bidding him the time of day there. Maybe he'd be inside in the kitchen, there or more likely sitting out here, and I'd say to him, "Hello there, Mr. Wilson"—you know the way, when you're going with a woman, you try to be affable to her aul fella—and he'd say, "Oh, hello there, Andy," or something like that back. But you know yourself, a man that's looking through binoculars, you don't like interrupting him. Civil wee man he was, too. Fifty years a stoker out in the general hospital. And a funny thing —one of the male nurses out there was telling me— all his life he stuck to the night shift: worked all night and slept all day, up there in that room above the kitchen. Peculiar, eh? All his life. Never saw the wife except maybe for a couple of hours in the evening. Never saw Hanna, the daughter, except at the weekends. Funny, eh? And yet by all accounts the civilest and decentest wee man you could meet. Funny, too. And the way things turn out in life; when the mother-in-law found him out here about seven o'clock that evening, she got such a bloody fright that she collapsed and took to the bed for good and hasn't risen since, not even the morning we got married. The heart. But that's another story. Anyway, Hanna and me, as I say,

we were only started going at the time; and then
with the aul fella dying and the aul woman taking to
the bed, like we couldn't go out to the pictures nor
dances nor nothing like any other couple; so I started
coming here every evening. And this is where we done
our courting, in there, on the couch. (*Chuckles
briefly.*) By God, we were lively enough, too. Eh? I
mean to say, people think that when you're . . . well,
when you're over the forty mark, that you're passified.
But aul Hanna, by God, I'll say that for her, she was
keen as a terrier in those days. (*Chuckles at the mem-
ory.*) If that couch could write a book—Shakespeare,
how are you! (*He rises from the chair.*) Every evening,
after I'd leave the workshop, I'd go home to my own
place at Riverview and wash myself down and make a
sup of tea and put on the good suit and call in at
Boyce's paper shop and get a quarter of clove rock—
that's the kind she liked—and come on over here and
there she'd be, waiting for me, in a gray skirt and a blue
jumper, and when she'd open the door to me, honest
to God the aul legs would damn near buckle under me.

HANNA *comes into the kitchen from upstairs. She is
dressed in a gray skirt and blue jumper.* ANDY *walks
through the invisible walls, through the hall, and taps on
the kitchen door.*

HANNA *is in her late forties. She works in a local shirt
factory, lives alone with her invalided mother, and until
ANDY came on the scene has not been out with a man for
over twenty years. And this sudden injection of romance
into a life that seemed to be rigidly and permanently*

patterned has transformed a very plain spinster into an almost attractive woman. With ANDY *she is warm: with her mother she reverts to waspishness.*

Because neither ANDY *nor* HANNA *is young, there is a curious and slightly dated diffidence between them. And yet, when they begin courting, it is* HANNA *who takes the initiative and caresses him with a vigor and concentration that almost embarrass him.*

ANDY: Well, Hanna.

HANNA: Hello, Andy.

ANDY: Not a bad evening.

HANNA: There's a cold wind, though.

ANDY: It's sharp—sharp.

HANNA: But it's nice all the same.

ANDY: Oh, very nice—very fresh. (*Pause.*) Nothing startling at the factory?

HANNA: Not a thing. Working away.

ANDY: Suppose so.

HANNA: Cutting out shirt collars this week. And you?

ANDY: Still at the furniture for the new hotel. Going to cost a fortune, yon place.

HANNA: I'll bet you.

ANDY: Only the very best of stuff going into it: maple and pine and mahogany. Lovely to work with.

HANNA: D'you see that now.

ANDY: Lovely.

Pause. Then ANDY *produces the small bag of sweets from his pocket.*

ANDY: Here. Catch.

He throws them to her.

HANNA: Oh, Andy . . .

ANDY: They don't even ask me in the shop any more. They just say, "Quarter pound of clove rock, Mr. Tracey. Right you are."

HANNA: You have me spoiled.

ANDY: How's the mother?

HANNA: (*Sharp*) Living. And praying.

ANDY: Terrible sore thing, the heart, all the same.

HANNA: I come home from my work beat out and before I get a bite in my mouth she says, "Run out like a good

child and get us a sprig of fresh flowers for Saint
Philomena's altar."

ANDY: Did you go?

HANNA *points to the flowers wrapped in paper lying on
the kitchen table.*

HANNA: But she can wait for them.

ANDY: She'll miss you when you leave, Hanna.

HANNA: Hasn't she Cissy Cassidy next door? And if she
hadn't a slavey like me to wait hand and foot on her,
her heart mightn't be just as fluttery!

*From behind the screen comes the sound of a bell—
not a tinkling little bell, but a huge brass bell with a long
wooden handle.*

We're early at it the night! There's the paper. Have a
look at it.

*With a bad grace she goes to answer the summons. As
she is about to exit:*

ANDY: The flowers.

She grabs them, grimaces, and leaves. ANDY *calls after
her:*

Tell Saint Philomena I was asking for her!

He chuckles at HANNA's *bad humor. Then he comes down stage and addresses the audience.*

That bloody bell! And nine times out of ten, you know, she didn't want a damn thing: Who's at the door? Is the fire safe? Did the Angelus ring? Is it time for the Rosary? Any excuse at all to keep Hanna on the hop, and at the same time making damn sure we weren't going to enjoy ourselves. But we got cute to her. You see, every sound down here carries straight up to her room; and we discovered that it was the long silences made her suspicious. That's the way with a lot of pious aul women—they have wild dirty imaginations. And as soon as there was a silence down here, she thought we were up to something and reached for the bloody bell. But if there was the sound of plenty chatting down here, she seldom bothered you. But I mean to say, if you're courting a woman there, you can't keep yapping about the weather all night. And it was the brave Hanna that hit on the poetry idea. Whenever we started the courting, she made me recite the poetry—you know there, just to make a bit of a noise. And the only poetry I ever learned at school was a thing called *Elegy Written in a Country Churchyard* by Thomas Gray, 1716 to 1771, if you ever heard tell of it. And I used to recite that over and over again. And Hanna she would throw an odd word in there to make it sound natural. And, by God, we'd hammer away at it until we'd stop for breath or for a sup of tea

or something; or else we'd get carried away and forget
the aul woman altogether—and then the bloody bell
would go and the session would be destroyed. But
they were good times . . . Funny thing about that
poem, too: it had thirty-two verses, and as long as I
could bull straight at it—you know, without thinking
what I was saying—I could rattle it off like a man. But
stop me in the middle of it or let me think of what I was
saying, and I had to go right back to the beginning
and start all over again. Christ, they were rare times,
too . . .

HANNA *returns.*

ANDY: Well?

HANNA: "Is that Andrew I hear?" "No," says I, "it's Jack
the Ripper."

ANDY: And how's Saint Philomena?

HANNA: You can laugh. "The pair of you'll be up later
for the Rosary, won't you?"

ANDY: (*Mock devotion*) With the help of God.

HANNA: One of these days I'll do something desperate.

*She sits dispiritedly beside him on the couch. He wants
to say something tender and consoling to her but feels
he is past the age for effusive, extravagant language.*

ANDY: You're looking nice, Hanna.

HANNA: It's the jumper.

Pause. Then he takes her hand in his and strokes it. She raises his hand to her lips and kisses it gently again and again. He puts his arm round her shoulder. They sit like this for some time.

We'd better keep talking.

ANDY: There's a nice smell of you.

HANNA: Soap.

ANDY: Nice soap.

HANNA: (*Dreamily*)   Her bloody ear'll be twitching like a rabbit.

ANDY: Hanna . . .

Pause. They speak the next eight lines as if they were in a trance.

HANNA: Say something, Andy.

ANDY: I don't want to.

HANNA: Please, Andy. She'll know.

ANDY: I don't give a damn.

HANNA: Andy . . .

ANDY: Nice . . .

HANNA: Please, Andy . . .

ANDY: Very nice . . .

Very suddenly, almost violently, HANNA *flings herself on him so that he falls back, and she buries her face in his neck and kisses and caresses him with astonishing passion. He is momentarily at a loss. But this has happened before, many times, and he knows that this is his cue to begin his poem. His recitation is strained and too high and too loud—like a child in school memorizing meaningless facts. Throughout his recital, they court feverishly.*

ANDY:

"The curfew tolls the knell of parting day,
The lowing herd wind slowly o'er the lea,
The plowman homeward plods his weary way,
And leaves the world to darkness and to me.
Now fades the glimmering landscape on the sight—"

HANNA: (*To ceiling*) It's a small world, isn't it?

ANDY:

"Now fades the glimmering landscape on the sight,
And all the air a solemn stillness holds,

Save where the beetle wheels his droning flight,
And drowsy tinklings lull the distant folds—"
Oh, God, Hanna—

HANNA: Just imagine. Fancy that. Keep going, man.

ANDY:
"Save that from yonder ivy-mantled tow'r
The moping owl does to the moon complain
Of such as, wand'ring near her secret bow'r,
Molest her ancient solitary reign."

HANNA: Andy—Andy—

ANDY: "Beneath those rugged elms, that yew-tree's shade—"

HANNA *groans voluptuously.*

ANDY: Steady on—steady on—say something—

HANNA: Mm?

ANDY: She'll be listening to—

HANNA: I don't give a damn.

ANDY: (*To ceiling*) Fine. Yes, indeed. Imagine that. Where in the name of God was I?

HANNA: "That yew-tree's shade—"

ANDY: What, where?

HANNA: "Beneath those rugged elms."

ANDY:
Oh. "Beneath those rugged elms, that yew-tree's shade,
Where heaves the turf in many a mould'ring heap,
Each in his narrow cell for ever laid,
The rude Forefathers of the hamlet sleep."
Speak, woman!

She kisses him on the mouth.

ANDY: Say something!

HANNA: Kiss me.

ANDY: For God's sake, woman—

HANNA: Andy, kiss me.

*He kisses her. They forget everything. The clanging of
the bell shatters the silence—and* HANNA *breaks away
roughly from him, jumps to her feet, and is almost trem-
bling with fury. Her jumper and skirt are twisted.*

HANNA: Bitch! The aul bitch!

ANDY: Sure you're only after leaving her! What the hell
can she want?

HANNA: Stuffed!

ANDY: Your jumper.

HANNA: Agh! My . . . !

She pulls the jumper right up and then pulls it back into place. ANDY *laughs at her anger.*

ANDY: Go on—go on—go on. A girl's best friend is her mother.

HANNA: Shut up, will you.

She adjusts her skirt and brushes back her hair and charges out of the room.
    ANDY *looks after her and smiles contentedly. Then he addresses the audience.*

ANDY: By God, she had spunk in those days, eh? Suited her, too: gave her face a bit of color and made her eyes dance. But whatever it was that happened to her —well, I mean to say, I think I know what happened . . . But, like, to see a woman that had plenty of spark in her at one time and then to see her turn before your very eyes into a younger image of her mother, by God it's strange, I'll tell you, very peculiar . . .

    But I was going to tell you about the aul woman and the altar and the Rosary and Saint Philomena and Father Peyton and all that caper. The routine was this.

At the stroke of ten every night wee Cissy Cassidy—
her and the aul woman's well met; two lisping Lizzies
—she came down and asked Hanna and me to go up
for the nightly Rosary. Fair enough. Why not? And
there's the aul woman lying in the bed, smiling like an
angel, and there, smiling back at her from the top of
a chest of drawers, is this big statue of Saint Philomena.
And you know, you got this feeling, with the flowers
and the candles lit and with all the smirking and
smiling and nodding and winking, you got the feeling
by God that you were up to the neck in some sort of a
deep plot or other. Like I knew damn well what the
aul woman was up to: if she couldn't break it up between Hanna and me, at least she was going to make
damn sure that I wasn't going to take Hanna away
from her. And *she* knew that *I* knew what she was
up to with her wee sermons about Father Peyton and
all the stuff about the family that prays together stays
together. And there was the pair of us, watching and
smiling, each of us knowing that the other knew, and
none of us giving away anything. By God, it was
strange. Eh? 'Cos she thought that every time I got
down on my knees in that bedroom to join in the
Rosary I was cutting my own throat. But because I
knew what she was up to, I was safe . . . or at least
I thought I was. She's crafty, that aul woman. You've got
to hand it to her. By God she's crafty.

*He goes upstage and casually lifts the newspaper to
glance over it.*

HANNA *enters on her way through to the scullery. She is carrying her mother's soiled tray.*

HANNA: Look at—the invalid tray! Not a crumb on it! Six rounds of a sliced-pan and a boiled egg! Thanks be to God she gets no fresh air or she'd eat up the town!

Knock at the front door.

That'll be prissy Cissy.

She goes off to the scullery. ANDY *goes to open the door.* CISSY *and* ANDY *come back to the kitchen briefly before* CISSY *goes upstairs.*
    CISSY *is a small, frail wisp of a woman in her late sixties. She lives next door, is a daily visitor, and because of the close friendship between herself and* MRS. WILSON *she has a proprietary air in this house. A lifetime spent lisping pious platitudes has robbed them of all meaning. The sickly piousity she exudes is patently false.*

ANDY: Hello, Cissy.

CISSY: Good night, Andrew. You're not alone, are you?

ANDY: Hanna's inside. How's things, Cissy?

CISSY: Struggling away, Andrew, thanks be to God. Sure as long as we have our health.

ANDY: That's it, Cissy.

CISSY: Thanks be to God, indeed. I'll go on up then, Andrew.

ANDY: Right—right.

CISSY: You'll be up later for the prayers?

ANDY: Aye.

CISSY: Thanks be to God.

HANNA *enters from the scullery. She is abrupt with* CISSY.

CISSY: Hello, Hanna. How's Mammy tonight?

HANNA: As ever.

CISSY: Sure that's grand.

ANDY: (*Winking at* HANNA) Thanks be to God.

CISSY: Just, Andrew—thanks be to God. Well . . . I'll see you both at ten.

ANDY: Joyful mysteries tonight, Cissy, isn't it?

CISSY: Thursday—so it is! Oh, you're coming closer and closer to us, Andrew Tracey!

She leaves. ANDY *laughs.*

HANNA: Sweet wee wasp!

HANNA *flops down on the couch.* ANDY *sits beside her. He sees she is in bad form and tries to coax her out of it.*

ANDY: Tired?

HANNA: Done out.

ANDY: D'you think was Cissy ever courted?

HANNA: Who cares?

HANNA: Imagine a man putting a hand on her knee. "Thanks be to God, mister."

She does not laugh.

You're in bad aul form, Hanna.

He puts his arm round her. She jumps to her feet.

HANNA: Not now.

ANDY: What's wrong? Is there something the matter?

HANNA: Sick—sick—sick—sick of the whole thing; that's what's the matter! I can't stand it much longer!

ANDY: Take a clove rock, Hanna.

HANNA: What in the name of God are we going to do?

ANDY: I've asked you half a dozen times to—

HANNA: It's her I'm talking about! Her up there! What do we do with her?

ANDY: When we're married she can come with us to Riverview. I've said that all—

HANNA: Never! Never! The day I get married I'm getting shot of her for good!

ANDY *spreads his hands: "What can I reply to that," the gesture says.*

And no matter what you say now, you know fine well you don't want her hanging round your neck either.

ANDY: I hear they took old Maggie Donaldson into Saint Patrick's.

HANNA: She's not sick enough for hospital. And they've no spare beds for cranks.

ANDY: The Nazareth nuns! Let her sell this place and go into the Nazareth House with the money.

HANNA: She wouldn't go to them above all people.

ANDY: What else is there?

HANNA: I don't know, Andy. Honest to God, I just don't know.

Pause, and it dawns on ANDY *that an offer is expected from him. He reacts strongly to the unspoken idea.*

ANDY: Well, damnit all, you don't expect me to come in here, do you? I mean to say, I have a place and all of my own, ready and furnished and everything! And leaping sky-high every time you hear a bloody bell isn't my idea of married bliss! My God, you don't expect that of me, do you? Well, do you?

HANNA: Bitch! That's what she is—an aul bitch!

ANDY: We're getting no younger, Hanna, you know.

HANNA: Tomorrow—I'll tell her tomorrow that we're going to clear out and she can damn well forage for herself!

ANDY: You'll like it over at Riverview. It's—it's—(*He sees that she is crying.*) Hanna, Hanna—aw, God, you're not away crying, are you—

He puts his arm round her and leads her to the couch. They sit. She blows her nose while he tries to console her.

ANDY: Come on, come on, there's no need for that. You know I can't stand seeing you crying. And you know

I'd do anything to make you happy. We'll solve it
some way or other. Don't you worry about it—we'll get
some solution to it all.

ANDY: . . . some solution to it all.

HANNA: No, we won't.

ANDY: I'm telling you we will.

HANNA: No, no. And only this morning I found myself
singing at my work. And sure I can't even sing in tune.

ANDY: I could listen to you all day.

HANNA: But sure nobody goes through life singing all
the time.

ANDY: We will, Hanna.

Very suddenly, almost violently—exactly as before—
HANNA *flings herself on him and smothers him with kisses.
And as before, he is taken unawares. Then he responds.
But after a few seconds he realizes that they are being
silent and launches into his poem.*

"The curfew tolls the knell of parting day,
　The lowing herd wind slowly o'er the lea,
　The plowman homeward plods his weary way,
　And leaves the world to darkness and to me."
Hanna . . . !

She does not hear him. Pause. Then he goes on.

"Now fades the glimmering landscape on the sight,
  And all the air a solemn stillness holds,
  Save where the beetle wheels his droning flight,
  And drowsy tinklings lull the distant folds."
Say something, woman!

HANNA: A loaf of bread costs 1/3½ and a pound of tea
  6/8.

ANDY:
  "Full many a gem of purest ray serene
  The dark unfathom'd caves of ocean bear:
  E'en from the tomb the voice of Nature cries—"
I've bucked it!

HANNA: "Can storied urn or animated bust—"

ANDY: What—what—what is it?

HANNA: "Back to its mansion call the fleeting breath."

ANDY:
  ". . . call the fleeting breath?
  Can Honour's voice provoke the silent dust,
  Or Flatt'ry soothe the dull cold ear of death?
  Perhaps in this neglected spot is laid
  Some heart once pregnant with celestial fire;
  Hands, that the rod of empire might have swayed . . ."

But he fades out because he can no longer resist the barrage of her passion. Their mouths meet. A long kiss. Silence. Then—the bell. HANNA *springs to her feet. This time* ANDY *is angry too.*

HANNA: Christ!

ANDY: For God's sake!

HANNA: Bitch! Bitch! Bitch! Bitch! Bitch!

ANDY: It's your fault! You make no attempt at all!

HANNA: I don't know no poems!

ANDY: Well . . . bloody shopping lists . . . multiplication tables . . . anything!

Again the bell.

What the hell can she want? Isn't Cissy with her?

HANNA: (*Evenly*) One of these days I'm going to strangle that woman . . . with her Rosary beads.

She marches off. ANDY *grabs a paper and tries to read it. We now see* HANNA *enter the bedroom and we hear* MRS. WILSON'S *voice.*

MRS. WILSON: We're going to say the Rosary a bit earlier tonight, dear. Cissy has a bit of a headache.

HANNA *removes the screen and puts it to the side of the set. In the large iron bed, propped up against the pillows, lies* MRS. WILSON. *Like* CISSY, *she is a tiny woman, with a sweet, patient, invalid's smile. Her voice is soft and commanding. Her silver hair is drawn back from her face and tied with a blue ribbon behind her head. She looks angelic.*

CISSY, *her understudy, is sitting beside her, watching her with devotion.*

Directly facing MRS. WILSON *is a chest of drawers, on which are a white cloth, two candles, a large statue of a saint, and a vase of flowers—a miniature altar.* MRS. WILSON *frequently nods and smiles to the statue and mouths "Thank you, thank you."* HANNA *clumps around the room, doing her chores with an ungracious vigor and with obvious ill-will.*

HANNA: Whatever suits Cissy suits me!

CISSY: She's looking lovely tonight, Hanna, isn't she? It must be the good care you're taking of her.

MRS. WILSON: I'm blessed, Cissy dear, and I know it. A good daughter is a gift of God. (*To the statue*) Thank you. (*To* HANNA, *who is fixing the bed clothes too robustly*) That's fine, dear, thank you. Just fine.

HANNA: Pillows.

MRS. WILSON: What's that, dear?

HANNA: D'you want me to beat up the pillows?

MRS. WILSON: No, I'm grand. A wee bit of discomfort's good for me.

CISSY: Invalids is all saints—that's what I say.

MRS. WILSON: Here's the matches, dear.

HANNA *goes and lights the candles.*

MRS. WILSON: Cissy, could I trouble you to give Andrew a call?

CISSY: Pleasure.

MRS. WILSON: (*To* HANNA) And maybe you'd be good enough to move Saint Philomena round a wee bit so that she's facing me . . . just a little to the left . . . so that we're looking at each other . . . That's it. Lovely. Thank you, dear.

CISSY *off and unseen.*

CISSY: Andrew!

MRS. WILSON: God be praised a thousand times. Saint Vibiana, Virgin and Martyr, protect us. Saint Hyacintha de Mariscottis, look after us this day and this night.

CISSY: The Rosary!

ANDY: Coming.

MRS. WILSON: (*To* HANNA) And my jewels, dear.

HANNA: What are you saying?

MRS. WILSON: Could you hand me my beads, please?

HANNA *does this.*

God bless you. Another day is nearly o'er. A journey closer to the heavenly shore.

Enter CISSY.

CISSY: He's coming. Thanks be to God.

MRS. WILSON: Amen to that. Poor Hanna's run off her feet, isn't she?

CISSY: A labor of love.

ANDY *enters. He tries to be brisk and matter-of-fact in this cloying feminine atmosphere.*

MRS. WILSON: Ah, Andrew!

ANDY: How are you tonight, Mrs. Wilson?

MRS. WILSON: Grand, Andrew, thanks. I have Saint Philomena during the day and I have you all at night.

ANDY: Very nice.

MRS. WILSON: Are you going to join us in the prayers?

HANNA: Didn't you send down for him!

MRS. WILSON: Thank you, Andrew. As Father Peyton says: the family that prays together stays together.

HANNA: Get started.

MRS. WILSON: And Father Peyton is right, isn't he, Andrew?

ANDY: Right, Mrs. Wilson.

MRS. WILSON: If you only knew the consolation it is for me to have you all kneeling round my bed.

CISSY: It's what you deserve.

MRS. WILSON: Thank you, Saint Philomena. Thank you.

HANNA: Who's giving it out?

MRS. WILSON: Aren't the flowers pretty, Andrew?

ANDY: Very nice.

MRS. WILSON: Hanna got them for me. But then—why wouldn't she? Didn't she take the name Philomena for her confirmation.

HANNA: Lookat—are we going to say the prayers or are we not?

CISSY: Hanna dear, you're talking to a sick woman.

MRS. WILSON *lays a restraining hand on* CISSY.

MRS. WILSON: She's tired, Cissy. I know. I don't mind. Maybe you'd give it out tonight, Andrew, would you?

ANDY: I—I—I—

HANNA: He will not, then. I will.

MRS. WILSON *mouths her thanks to the statue.* HANNA *begins at top speed.*

HANNA: In the name of the Father and of the Son and of the Holy Ghost. We fly to thy protection, O holy mother of God. Despise not our prayers in our necessity, but deliver us from all dangers, O glorious and ever blessed virgin. Thou O Lord will open my lips.

OTHERS: And my tongue shall announce thy praise.

HANNA: Incline unto my aid, O God.

OTHERS: O Lord, make haste to help me.

HANNA: Glory be to the Father and to the Son and to the Holy Ghost.

OTHERS: As it was in the beginning, is now, and ever shall be, world without end, Amen.

They are all on their knees around the bed, facing the altar now. While the prayers continue, ANDY *gets to his feet and places the screen in its opening position—that is, completely hiding the bedroom. He then goes behind the screen to continue the Rosary.*
The lights come down slowly and the prayers fade. Total black for about a minute.

When the lights go up, ANDY *is sitting as we first saw him, in the back yard, with his binoculars. He leaves down the binoculars, glances cautiously over his shoulder at the kitchen to make sure that no one in the house over-hears him, and then speaks to the audience.*

ANDY: The big mistake I made was to come back here after the honeymoon—*even* for the couple of weeks that it was supposed to be at the beginning. I should have put the foot down then. But, like, everything happened so sudden. One bright morning the firm turns round and says "All the single men in the joinery room are being sent to Belfast on a contract job." So there was nothing for it, like, but to get married. And that's what we done. And then when we got back from the three days in Dublin, there's the damn painters still hashing about in Riverview, and the aul woman has a bit of a flu, and Hanna's kind of worried about her, and damnit, between one thing and another we find ourselves back here. But it was to have been only

for a couple of weeks—that was the arrangement—
aw, no, there was no doubt about that. Two weeks,
she said. And a funny thing, you know, looking back
on it, there was a change in the tune even then. No,
not so much with the aul woman—she's too cratty—
Christ, you've got to hand it to the aul woman—but
with Hanna. Like, you know, before we got married,
she was full of fight, there: let the aul woman step out
of line or say something sharp to me and by God she
jumped at her like a cock at a gooseberry. But somehow the spirit seemed to drain out of her from the
very beginning. Of course, when the bloody bell would
go, she would still say, "The aul bitch!" But, you know,
even the way she said it now, like kind of weary, and
almost as if it wasn't anger at the aul woman at all but
more to please me. That sort of thing. And a funny
thing about that bloody bell, too. You know, before, if
there was no noise coming from downstairs, that ringing would be enough to waken the dead. But *after*
we got married, it only went when Hanna and me
started talking. Wasn't that perverse now, eh? Oh, a
deep one; deep as a well. We could sit, by God, for a
whole night and not say a word to other, and there
wouldn't be a cheep from upstairs. But let us start
chatting and the clanging would damn near shake the
house! You know there, that sort of thing.

And then there was the Rosary caper. Well, I mean
to say, a man has to draw the line somewhere. Oh, no,
says I; we may have to stay together of necessity, says
I, but by God it won't be because we pray together;
I'll say my own mouthful of prayers down here. And

that settled that. I mean to say, a man has to take a
stand some time. No harm to Father U. S. A. Peyton,
says I; but all things in their proper place, and the
proper place for me and my missus is in Riverview.
I'll manage rightly down here, says I; and Father
Peyton and Saint Philomena and the three sorrowful
mysteries can hammer away upstairs. She didn't like
that, the aul woman, I'll tell you. Didn't speak to me
for weeks. And would you believe what she done on
me to get her own back: it was Cissy told me with a
wee toss of her head. "She offered you up to Saint
Philomena," says she. Crafty? Oh, man! Hanna's thick—
there's no denying that; but she'll never have the craft
of the aul woman.

But I got her! By God I got her! . . . or I damn near
got her. It was this day in the works—a Friday—I'll
never forget it—and George Williamson comes sidling
up to me with a newspaper in his hand and a great aul
smirk on his jaw, and says he, "So the Pope's not in-
fallible after all, Andy," says he. Oh, a bad bitter
Protestant, the same Williamson. "What's that?" says
I, you know there, very quiet. "According to the
paper here," says he, "even the Pope can make a mistake. What d'you make of that now, eh? Isn't that a
surprise?" And he hands me the paper. So I pulls out
the glasses, very calm, and puts them on, and takes the
paper from him and looks at it. And true as Christ,
when I seen it, you could have tipped me over, I was
that weak. Like, for five seconds, I couldn't even speak
with excitement; only the heart thumping like bloody
hell in my chest. For there it was in black and white

before my very eyes: THE SAINT THAT NEVER WAS. "Official Vatican sources today announced"—I know it by heart—"that the devotion of all Roman Catholics to Saint Philomena must be discontinued at once because there is little or no evidence that such a person ever existed." Like I never knew I was a spiteful man until that minute; and then, by God, my only thought was to stick that paper down the aul woman's throat. Poor Williamson—Christ, I shot past him like a scalded cat and out of the workshop like the hammers of hell.

What I should have done—like, I know now—my God, no need to tell me; instead of coopering the thing up the way I done—but what I should have done was wait until after the tea and then go upstairs nice and calm, you know there, and sit down on the side of the bed very pleasant, and say, "Have a look through the paper there, Mrs. Wilson," and watch, by God, watch every wee flicker of her eye when she'd come to the big news . . . but I bollixed it. I know. I know. I bollixed it. Straight from the workshop into a pub. And when closing time comes, there I am— blotto. And back to the house singing and shouting like a madman.

HANNA, *who has been in the bedroom, now removes the screen. And, as she does this,* ANDY *goes off.*

MRS. WILSON *is in bed.* CISSY *is sitting on the edge of the bed.* HANNA *has been crying for some time and shuffles around the room, vaguely touching different things.*

The candles are lit.

The atmosphere is subdued and doleful and expectant. Trite words of consolation are being spoken. And one gets the sense of feminine solidarity and of suffering womanhood.

MRS. WILSON: I promise you, dear: he's all right. I know he is.

HANNA: But where *is* he?

MRS. WILSON: Maybe he met some of his companions.

HANNA: He has no companions.

MRS. WILSON: Maybe he's doing overtime.

HANNA: There's no overtime this week.

MRS. WILSON: Or maybe he's gone to confession.

CISSY: Ah! Indeed!

HANNA: At half past ten? For God's sake!

MRS. WILSON: Well, we'll say the Rosary; that's what we'll do; and we'll ask God and Saint Philomena to look after us all. And before we're finished, you'll find he'll be home safe and sound to us.

CISSY: Thanks be to God.

MRS. WILSON: All down on your knees. God and his holy
mother guide all our thoughts and actions this day and
this night. In the name of the Father and of the Son
and of the Holy Ghost. The five sorrowful mysteries
of the most holy Rosary—

Remote sounds of ANDY *singing.*

HANNA: Sshhh!

MRS. WILSON: The first sorrowful mystery—the agony in
the garden—

HANNA: Sh! Sh! Listen! Listen!

The women freeze. Downstairs ANDY *staggers into the
kitchen, singing* God Save Ireland. *The women are hor-
rified.*

MRS. WILSON: Is it—?

HANNA: Shut up!

CISSY: Singing! Andrew?

MRS. WILSON: He's not—?

HANNA: He is!

CISSY: A drunk man!

ANDY *flings his coat on the couch and reels to the bottom of the stairs. Calls up:*

ANDY: Mrs. Wilson! Hello there, old mammy Wilson! I've got news for you . . . big, big news.

HANNA *is terrified.* MRS. WILSON *takes control.*

HANNA: What in the name of God—?

MRS. WILSON: Leave him to me.

ANDY: Stay where you are till I come up . . . very important, old mammy . . . very important.

MRS. WILSON: Don't say a word. Leave everything to me.

CISSY: Drunk—the dirty animal!

MRS. WILSON: Quiet.

HANNA: But what if he—?

MRS. WILSON: Don't worry. I'll settle him. And stop whining!

ANDY *enters and surveys the three alarmed faces. He has the newspaper in his hand.*

ANDY: By God if it's not the Dolly Sisters! (*He gives them a grand bow.*) And Saint Philomena! (*Grand bow*

to the statue.) All we need now is Father Peyton . . .
Where's Father Peyton? . . . I'll tell you something: the
family that drinks together sinks together.

MRS. WILSON: Andrew!

ANDY: "The cock's shrill clarion, or the echoing horn—"

CISSY: Dirty animal!

ANDY:
"No more shall rouse them from their lowly bed.
 For them no more the blazing hearth shall burn,
 Or busy housewife ply her evening care—"
Thomas Gray, 1716 to 1771.

HANNA: Mother, please—!

MRS. WILSON: Listen to me, Andrew!

ANDY: She (HANNA) knows what I'm talking about 'cos
she's my wife—

MRS. WILSON: If you don't behave yourself—

ANDY: As for prissy Cissy here—

CISSY: All for Thee—all for Thee—

ANDY: You'll go down with the white bobbins. Know
what that means, prissy Cissy? The white bobbins? It
means you'll never know your ass from your elbow.

HANNA: Andy!

MRS. WILSON: I'll give you one minute to get out of this house—!

ANDY: News for you, old mammy—here, in this paper. (*To the statue*) And news for you, darling, too.

MRS. WILSON: Get out!

ANDY: You've (PHILOMENA) been sacked.

MRS. WILSON: I said get out!

ANDY: (*To statue*) You and me—both sacked.

He comes over to the bed with the paper.

HANNA: Stop it, Andrew! Stop it!

ANDY: In black and white . . . Read it . . . It says: We don't stay together—that's what it says. Father Peyton, it says, your head's a marly. That's what it says.

CISSY: Dirty, dirty animal.

MRS. WILSON: I warned you! I gave you ample warning! And if you think you can profane in this room—

She breaks off and clutches her heart and cries out.

CISSY: What—what is it?

HANNA: Mother! Mother!

ANDY *staggers back to the altar. On his way he kicks over the bell. He laughs.*

ANDY: "The curfew tolls no more the knell of parting day." (*He lifts the statue and waltzes with it.*) Come on, darling; we know when we're not wanted.

MRS. WILSON: Don't—touch—that—

CISSY: The statue!

HANNA: Andrew!

CISSY: Oh, my God!

MRS. WILSON: Stop him! Stop him!

Chaos and confusion as HANNA *and* CISSY *rush at* ANDY *and wrest the statue from him. Everyone is shouting at the same time.* MRS. WILSON *gets out of bed and* CISSY *puts a coat round her.*

CISSY: Come on! Come on! Into my place!

HANNA: Are you all right, Mother?

ANDY:

"Large was his bounty, and his soul sincere,
Heav'n did a recompense as largely send—"

MRS. WILSON: Take all—statue—candles—cloth—

CISSY: Brute animal!

MRS. WILSON: Oh, my heart—

HANNA: Out—quick—

CISSY *and* HANNA *each take an arm of* MRS. WILSON *and
they support her out.* HANNA *also takes the altar things.*
MRS. WILSON *groans loudly and pathetically.* CISSY *con-
soles her.* ANDY *reels over to the bed and sits on it. He is
muttering to himself.* HANNA *leaves the others, goes to
him, and sticks her face into his, and hisses:*

HANNA: You'll regret this day, Andrew Tracey! You'll
regret this day as long as you live!

She then pulls over the screen hiding ANDY *from view,
and joins* CISSY *and her mother, who go off chattering
hysterically.* ANDY *rises and watches them go. He shouts
after them.*

ANDY: (*Shouts after them from behind the screen*)
We're sacked, Philomena—both of us—both sacked!
What the hell are we going to do now? What the hell
are we going to do now?

*The three women have struggled downstairs and pause
in the kitchen before escaping to* CISSY'S *house.*

WILSON: Oh my heart! O my God!

HANNA: How are you, Mother?

CISSY: All men is animals—brute animals.

HANNA: Come on, Mother. I'll look after you.

CISSY: Brutes of the field.

MOTHER: God have mercy on us this day and this night.

HANNA: He'll pay for this. By God, he'll pay for this!

The three ladies go off.
ANDY *appears, in cardigan and house slippers, and
comes into the kitchen. He addresses the audience.*

ANDY: I don't think I told you about the tenant I have
over in Riverview. Retired accountant. Quiet couple.
No kids. He pays me on the first Saturday of every
month. Sometimes if the weather's good I take an odd
walk over there and look at the outside of the house.
He has rose trees in the front and vegetables at the
back. Very nice. Very cozy. But by the time you get
home from work and get washed, you don't feel like
going out much. So I usually sleep at the fire for a
while and then come out here for a breath of air.

Kills an hour or two. And then when the bell rings I go up to the aul woman's room for the prayers. Well, I mean to say, anything for a quiet life. Hanna sleeps there now, as a matter of fact, just in case the aul woman should get an attack during the night. Not that that's likely. The doctor says she'll go on forever.

And a funny thing, you know: nothing much has changed up there. Philomena's gone, of course. And she never mentions Father Peyton any more. But she still has the altar and she still lights the candles and has the flowers in the middle and she still faces it when she's praying and mouths away to it. I asked Cissy about it one night when she came in—who the hell they were supposed to be praying to.

Enter cissy *in coat and hat. She is about to go straight upstairs but sees* andy *and pauses. She is very formal with him.*

cissy: Good night, Andrew.

andy: 'Night, Cissy.

cissy: The crowds for confession! You should see them. The poor priests must be mortified.

andy: Cissy—

cissy: You'll be up later for the prayers?

andy: I will. I will. Cissy—

CISSY: Well?

ANDY: Cissy, you've no statue up there now.

CISSY: I'm not blind.

ANDY: Well, I mean to say, what does she think she's at?

CISSY: We've no statue, true enough; but we have a saint in our mind even though we've no figure for it.

HANNA *enters.* ANDY *does not see her at first.*

ANDY: What saint?

CISSY: Aha, that's something you'll never know, Andrew Tracey! Wild horses wouldn't drag that out of us. You robbed us of Saint Philomena but you'll never rob us of this one, for you'll never be told who it is!

CISSY *marches upstairs and* ANDY *turns with embarrassment to* HANNA. *Her coldness to him is withering.*

ANDY: Damnit, she's fighting fit . . . isn't she? Hanna—

HANNA: What?

ANDY: Hanna, things are . . . we're not making . . . you and me, Hanna, we're not . . . Here, have a clove rock, Hanna.

*She moves toward him as if she were going to take one,
hesitates, then says:*

HANNA: No. They'd put me off my supper.

ANDY: I suppose you're right.

HANNA: You'll be up for the prayers?

ANDY: I will . . . I will . . .

HANNA *goes upstairs.* ANDY *turns to the audience and
speaks with strained joviality.*

ANDY: And that's the way things are now. (*He goes
slowly out toward the yard.*) And when I go into the
bedroom she smiles and nods at me and you can see her
lips saying *Thank you, thank you,* to the altar. And
when we kneel down, she says, "It's nice for me to have
you all gathered round my bed. As a certain American
cleric says: the family that prays together stays together."
    By God, you've got to admire the aul bitch. She could
handle a regiment.

*He lifts the binoculars, puts them in front of his eyes,
and stares at the wall in front of him.*
    *Slowly bring down the lights until the stage is totally
black.*